B is for Benye:

A Virgin Islands Historical and Cultural A-Z Book

Charlene Blake- Pemberton

Illustrated by: Ginelle Encarnacion

Halo
Publishing International

ISBN: 978-1-61244-342-3

Printed in the United States of America

Halo ● ● ● ●
Publishing International

Published by Halo Publishing International
1100 NW Loop 410
Suite 700 - 176
San Antonio, Texas 78213
Toll Free 1-877-705-9647
Website: www.halopublishing.com
E-mail: contact@halopublishing.com

This book is dedicated to my grandson, Andrew Francis. My hope is that through this book he will learn about his history and culture. And that someday he will pass down Virgin Islands history to his children.

ACKNOWLEDGEMENTS

For their help with this book, I express grateful thanks to the following: Edna G. Thomas; Yvette M Arnold; Olive A Walcott; Felicia Rogers; Jillian Rose; Dmitri Copeman; Janice Tutein; Salad and Words Writing Group; Opal Palmer Adisa; Daisy Lafond; Pat Brown and Mike Taras of cpmvi.com.

Special Thank You to: James Pemberton and to my daughter Jaynelle Pemberton.

Thank you for reading my manuscripts over and over; thank you for always believing in me and making sure I got my book published.

INTRODUCTION

"There are two gifts we should give our children: one is roots and the other is wings." - Hodding Carter

The US Virgin Islands was once known as the Danish West Indies, a major sugar producing area. In the past the flags of Spain, England, Holland, France, The Knights of Malta and Denmark once flew over the island of St. Croix. Because of these influences, Virgin Islanders are always eager to share this unique blend of culture.

During World War I, The United States purchased the Virgin Islands. On March 31, 1917, the official transfer took place. After the transfer, the islands of St. Croix, St. Thomas and St. John became the Virgin Islands of the United States.

This book is for the children of the Virgin Islands so they can learn about their roots, which include the contributions of many important Virgin Islanders and other unique traditions of their home-land. Also, it is for you, our visitors to the islands, so you can discover who we are and share what you learn about us with your family and friends abroad.

B is for Benye: A Virgin Islands Historical and Cultural A-Z Book begins with a Virgin Islands family, the Penns, living In Orlando Florida. The grandparents, Clarice and Vincent, who live on the island of St. Croix, want to pass down and share their Virgin Islands heritage with their grandchildren,

Madelyn and Joah who have visited St. Croix only one time. So, both grandparents decided to send the children a very special present.

Can you guess what present the Penns sent their grandchildren?

Well, come along and find out.

Madelyn and Joah arrived home from school with their dad and discovered a package by their front door.

Picking up the box, Joah said, "It's a package from Grandpa in St. Croix!"

"Open it! Open it!" yelled Madelyn, his younger sister.

Joah and Madelyn finding a package at the front door.

"Let's do that inside," said their dad, opening the door and holding it for them to enter.

Both children sprinted into the house and headed straight to the kitchen. Joah placed the box on the table.

Madelyn perched close to her brother while he ripped off the paper and pried the box opened.

"It's a book and a Kindle!"Joah bellowed, holding one in each of his hand.

Madelyn grabbed the book from Joah, admiring the pictures. Joah pushed the button on the Kindle and waited for the screen to focus. He peered at the screen.

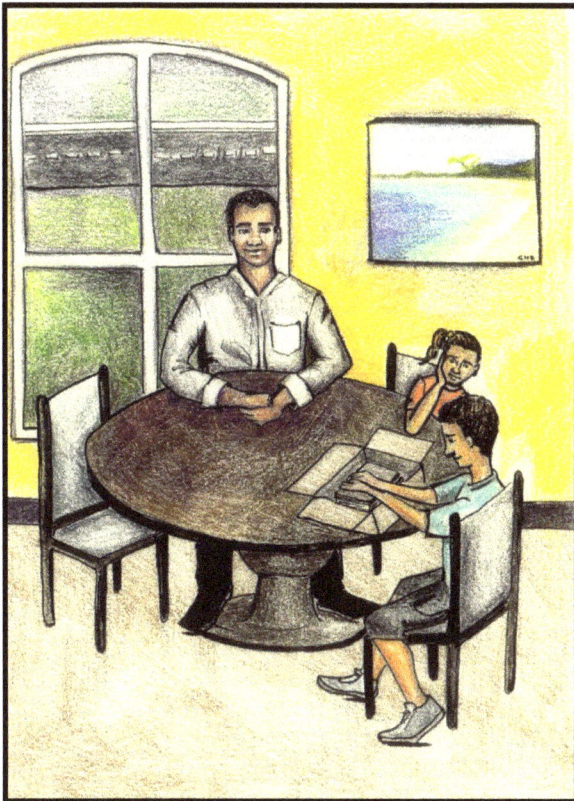

Dad, Madelyn and Joah opening the package.

"B is for Be, Ben... Dad, what's this word?" Joah moved the screen so his father could see it.

"Benye," said his dad, a smile on his face. "Your grandmother makes the best benye in all of St Croix."

"What's a benye?" both children chimed.

"I bet if you continue reading you will find out," answered their father.

Madelyn opened the cover of her book.

Joah read, "B is for Benye: A Virgin Islands Historical and Cultural A-Z Book."

"Benye is history?" asked Madelyn, a puzzled look on her face.

"Dad, I thought you said benye was something Grandma makes?"

"It is," responded their dad, getting them to sit down. "But it's also the title for Grandma's book. Be patient and read on," said Dad sitting with the children.

Madelyn opened her book to A and Joah settled more comfortable on the chair and read aloud,

"A is for Alton A. Adams."

"Look, all the letters in his name begins with A," declared Madelyn, tracing the letters with her fingers.

"That's very observant," said her dad patting her on the head. "Continue reading," he nodded to Joah.

"Alton Augustus Adams Sr. was the first African Caribbean bandmaster admitted into the United States Navy. He directed the United States Navy Band of the Virgin Islands from 1917-1931. Under his direction the band received many tributes from the navy for its musical performances.

Used with permission granted by Alton A. Adams, Jr.

Alton A. Adams

Adams Sr. was born on November 4, 1889 on the island of St. Thomas, one of the three islands that make up the US Virgin Islands. His early musical interest stirred after he received a piccolo from his grandmother. Without formal training he learned to play this instrument, but later, when he was nine years old; he received music lessons from his teacher Jean Pierre. After turning seventeen years old, Alton Augustus Adams continued studying music from institutions abroad that offered classes through the mail because there weren't any high schools or colleges in St. Thomas at that time.

At age twenty one, he formed the Adams Juvenile Band. This band later became the US Navy Band of the Virgin Islands. While playing for the Navy, Adams composed several marches. One of them he named, *The Virgin Islands March*, which he composed in 1919.

In June of 1982 the march was adopted as the official anthem of the Virgin Islands."

"Your mother has a recording of *The Virgin Islands March*." I 'm sure she will play it for you when she comes home," their dad said as Madelyn turned her page and before she shouted, "B is for benye!"

Benye

"Benye is island bread made with ripe mashed bananas and island spices," continued Joah. "Traditionally, breakfast consisted of bush tea (lemon grass and basil) with bread. Years ago the benye lady walked the streets around 7 a.m. with these delicacies.

Although the islands were owned by the Danes, before the USA bought them, many people from France lived in the Virgin Islands, and they shared their culture. Numerous Virgin Islanders believed that benye, one of our local breads, is the island version of the French beignet (pronounced ben -yay). Today, this traditional treat is frequently prepared during food fairs and festivals throughout the islands."

"Look at the big ships in the port," shouted Madelyn shoving her book in front of Joah. "Your Kindle doesn't have pictures like this," she stated poking out her tongue.

"Yes it does. See for yourself."Joah put his Kindle on top of her book, a big grin on his face.

Madelyn glanced at the picture on the Kindle and then rolled her eyes.

"Let's see what else we learn about the Virgin Islands," interrupted Dad, refocusing both children.

Feeling satisfied, Joah continued reading.

"C is for Charlotte Amalie."

Charlotte Amalie

"Named in honor of a Danish queen Charlotte Amalie, the capital of the US Virgin Islands, is cuddled by little bays. In the 1800's, the town was once a shipping center and distributing site for the Caribbean. Charlotte Amalie today is a prospering sea port for many cruise ships."

"Are places named after princesses too?" asked Madelyn.

"No," said Dad while responding to a text message.

"Why not?" continued Madelyn with disappointment in her voice.

"Ask Dad after he comes off his cell phone," responded Joah.

"That was Mom. She is working late tonight, and we'll have to prepare a snack until she gets home. Who wants a fruit snack?" asked their dad.

"I'll have a banana and peanut butter sandwich," answered Joah.

"Me too," chimed Madelyn.

"Continue reading while I fix the snacks," his dad instructed.

"Oh, Madelyn wants to know if there are places honoring princesses on the islands."

"No," answered their father while removing a couple of bananas from the fruit bin.

"Why not?" asked Madelyn.

"The streets throughout the islands are mainly the names of kings and queens," replied her dad.

"How come?" insisted Madelyn.

"Well, a princess had to wait until she became a queen," stated her dad.

"Oh! A princess would have to wait until she grew up," Madelyn said with understanding.

"Yes, something like that," said her father while signaling for Joah to continue.

"D is for David Hamilton Jackson (1884-1946)," continued Joah.

David Hamilton Jackson

"As a labor leader, lawyer, journalist and judge, David Hamilton Jackson was dedicated to the struggle of his people. In 1915 Jackson organized the first labor union on St. Croix to fight for the rights of oppressed workers."

"What's a labor union?" asked Madelyn.

"That's when workers form a group for better pay and for better working conditions," responded her brother. "The workers wanted fair pay and David helped them get it."

Madelyn nodded yes and Joah found his place on the Kindle and continued.

"Jackson was born on St. Croix on September 28, 1884.

Because of his intellectual abilities, he was chosen in 1915 to represent his people in Denmark. While there, he asked the King and the Danish Parliament to give up government control of the press. He prevailed and in 1925 he established The Herald, the first independent newspaper in the Virgin Islands.

His accomplishment is remembered each year on November 1 in observance of freedom of the press.

David Hamilton Jackson died on May 30, 1946."

"Ok! It's snack time," yelled Dad as he led the children to the counter. "After eating, we can continue learning about our culture."

Madelyn and Joah raced to the white counter top in the kitchen. Both children flopped on the stools and began eating.

Madelyn and Joah eating.

After finishing their snacks, Dad cleared the counter while Joah and Madelyn returned to their seats by the dining table.

As he placed the dirty plates in the sink, Dad said, "Continue reading Joah."

Joah found his place in the Kindle and read, "E is for Melvin H. Evans."

"Melvin Herbert Evans had a brilliant career as a physician, governor, congressman and ambassador. Evans was born on August 7, 1917 on St. Croix.

After graduating from high school on St. Thomas, Evans received his Bachelor of Science degree from Howard University in 1940. Four years later, he received his Medical Doctor's degree from the Howard College of Medicine.

Melvin H. Evans

In 1944 when Dr. Evans returned home, Virgin Islanders were proud as he began his career in the medical field."

"Why were they proud?" asked Madelyn.

"Becoming a doctor is a great profession. Besides, he was a native Virgin Islander who had returned home to help his community," responded Dad. "In the 40's native doctors were few or nonexistent on St. Croix."

"Oh," said Madelyn as she settled into her chair.

Then Joah found his place in the Kindle and resumed reading.

"Twenty six years later, Evans entered the political arena.

Before 1970, governors in the US Virgin Islands were appointed by the president of the United States. However, in

1968 Congress passed the Virgin Islands Elective Governor Act. This law provided for the election of a governor by the residents of the Virgin Islands. Evans joined the governor's race in 1970, and he became the first elected governor of the U.S. Virgin Islands.

He later served in the Ninety-sixth Congress of the United States (January 3, 1979-January 3, 1981). In his last political appointment, he served as United States ambassador to Trinidad and Tobago."

"We can Google Dr. Evans later to find out more about his career," suggested Dad.

"Maybe I can write a report on Dr. Evans and introduce him to my history class," declared Joah.

"That's an excellent idea," said Dad as he signaled for him to continue.

"F is for Fife," read Joah.

Sketch By: John Jones

18

"Madelyn, before you ask what a fife is? Let me read the definition," said Joah.

Madelyn shuffled in her chair and waited impatiently for Joah to continue.

"The Fife is a wooden musical instrument," continued her brother. "Originally, early local musicians made fifes from bamboo sticks."

"Bamboo sticks are strong wood like material that is used to make furniture," inserted Dad. "The coffee table in our living room is made from bamboo."

Joah and Madelyn peeked into the living room and nodded in agreement. Then he found his place on the Kindle.

"The fife and drum bands can be traced back to slavery on the islands. Quelbe bands with fife players have serenaded the people and kept the musical culture alive on the islands."

"Quelbe is the native folk music of the Virgin Islands," added Dad. "You guys heard it when you visited Grandma and Grandpa."

Joah and Madelyn nodded yes in agreement.

"G is for Ginger Thomas," continued Joah as he curled his legs up on the chair.

Ginger Thomas

"Ginger Thomas is the island name for the Yellow Cedar tree. Tecoma Stans is the scientific name.

These sunny yellow flowers thrive year round covering the hillsides and backyards of homes in the Virgin Islands."

"They are the same color as the blouse Mom got for me!" shouted Madelyn.

"Yes," said Dad.

Madelyn chuckled and Joah found his place once again on the Kindle and continued reading.

"The Ginger Thomas was proclaimed the official national flower of the islands, by Governor Paul Pearson In 1934."

"H is for Alexander Hamilton," read Joah.

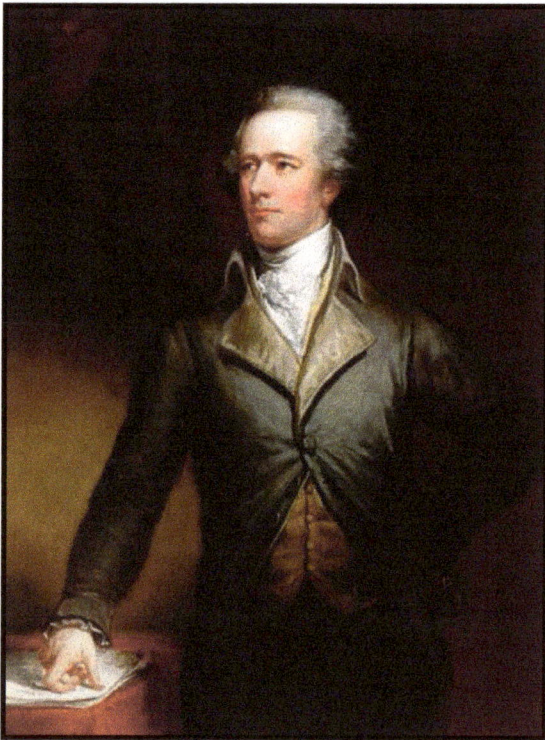

Alexander Hamilton, Picture in Public Domain.

"Alexander Hamilton grew up on the island of St. Croix. Young Hamilton worked as a clerk at a shipping company on the island."

"We read about Alexander Hamilton in history class. But, I don't remember reading that he came from St. Croix," said Joah looking puzzled.

"Actually, he was born on another island called Nevis, but he was raised on St. Croix," explained their father. "Let's continue reading to learn more."

"In 1773 friends and relatives on the island sent Hamilton to New York to receive formal education. After the American Revolution, he was selected by George Washington to be the first Secretary of the Treasury.

Alexander Hamilton came from humble beginnings and later became one of America's founding fathers. His portrait graces the American ten dollar bill."

"Why don't you Google Hamilton later and see what else you can find out about him?" suggested their dad. "Madelyn, what's the next letter?"

"I!"yelled Madelyn.

"I is for inkberry," read Joah.

"The inkberry stands around 5-10 feet with straight branches. It is the traditional Virgin Islands Christmas tree. In the past, families climbed the hills and chopped down their own inkberry trees. Decorated with homemade trinkets, the trees then stood on porches or in windows for all to see at Christmas time."

Photo Credit: University of the Virgin Islands, Cooperative Extension Service

Madelyn flipped the page and said, "It looks almost like our Christmas tree."

"Yeah! But, our trees don't have straight branches," said Joah, looking at her book.

"But it still looks like the one we have at Christmas time," insisted Madelyn.

"I'm a little tired from reading," yawned Joah.

"Let's take turns reading," said their dad, taking the Kindle from Joah. "That way, you can rest for a while."

"Can I read too?" asked Madelyn.

"Why don't you read the first sentences?" suggested Dad, as he sat closer to his two children. "Then I will read the other sentences."

"Ok!" said Madelyn as she spread her book wide and began reading.

"J is for Jose An-to-nio- Jar-vis."

"That's excellent!" said her father and he continued reading. "Antonio Jarvis is remembered as a poet, historian, educator and publisher. Jarvis published the first Daily News paper in 1930 on the island of St. Thomas. In the first edition he stated that he hoped 'it would serve as an inspiration to a city whose traditions go back two hundred years…'Eighty five years later the award winning Daily News is still published on St. Thomas.

Jose Antonio Jarvis

Jose Antonio Jarvis died on July 21, 1963."

"What does in-spi-ra-tion mean?" asked Madelyn.

"Well," said Dad. "It's like when Mom and I cheer for you at a soccer game. We encourage you to try harder. It is the same with the newspaper. Mr. Jarvis wanted the paper to encourage the people of the island."

"And it did!" injected Joah, "because it's still being printed."

"That's right son," said his dad as he pulled his chest slightly upward beaming with pride.

Then he scrolled the screen, and Madelyn read her sentence.

"K is for kal- la- loo," pronounced Madelyn.

"I sure love kallaloo," declared Dad as he continued reading.

Kallaloo

"Many in the Virgin Island celebrate the New Year with a bowl of kallaloo soup. Some on the islands believe that it brings good luck in the New Year. This native soup is made with the kallaloo bush, okra, spinach, salted pig's tail and seafood."

"I don't like pig's tail in my soup," declared Madelyn pinching her nose.

"You don't even taste it in the kallaloo," said her dad with a smile on his face. "All the ingredients are stewed right in with the greens. This is a popular dish found in many Virgin Islands kitchens."

Then Madelyn found her place in the book and read, "L is for lemon grass."

"As the name suggests lemon grass is a grass-like plant used to make tea," read Dad. "In the Virgin Islands, any herbs used to make tea are simply called bush tea. One of the most popular bush teas on the island is lemon grass.

Photo Credit: www.freedigitalphoto.net

Lemon Grass

This herb is known to aid digestion, reduce muscle cramps and relieve headaches. Chilled with ice, it is a refreshing lemon drink on a blistering Virgin Islands day."

"We had lemon grass tea when we visited last summer," declared Joah.

It was sweet and lemony," agreed Madelyn closing her eyes remembering the taste.

Dad then gestured for Madelyn to continue.

"M is for My-rah Kea-ting Smith."

Myra Keating Smith

"Myrah Keating Smith began her nursing education in Alabama," continued Dad. "After graduating with a degree in nursing and midwifery, she returned to the islands in 1931."

"A midwife is someone who is trained to deliver babies in a hospital or in a home," responded their father. Midwifery is the actual technique or procedure used by the midwife."

"Like what we saw on the TV show?" asked Joah.

"Yes, that's correct son," responded his dad as he scrolled the screen to find his place.

"For twenty years she was the only health care provider on St. John. Miss Myrah was the public health nurse, school nurse, registered nurse and midwife for the island.

For her service and dedication, the Virgin Islands named the health clinic on the island of St. John in her honor. Miss Myrah died in May 1994."

"N is for Na-tive Vir-gin Is-lan-der," continued Madelyn. "Are you a native Dad?" she asked.

Illustration by: Ginelle Encarnacion
Native Virgin Islanders

"Yes, I am. I was born on the island of St. Croix, and your mom was born on the island of St. Thomas," her dad said all smiles.

"Am I a native too?" she asked.

"You and your brother were born in Florida, so you all are natives of Florida; but, your roots are in the Virgin Islands," answered Dad.

"Oh," said Madelyn as she cuddled her book and waited for her father to continue reading.

"Native people inhabited the Virgin Islands long before Columbus arrived. These groups included the Arawaks, Ciboneys, Caribs, and Tainos Indians."

"Are you a native like the Indians?" asked Joah.

"The Indians were the real natives of the islands before Columbus' era," explained Dad. "After that time anyone born on the islands is considered a native.

In 1733 the Danes arrived and developed plantations for growing sugar cane. The enslaved Africans worked the sugar fields until the rebellion in 1848.

Various nationalities have left trademarks on the islands throughout the centuries," continued their dad. "However, today Virgin Islanders are largely of African descendants, with some European, East Indian, and Spanish ancestry.

Anyone born in the US Virgin Islands is a native. A native Virgin Islander always greets others with Good morning, Good afternoon, Good evening, or Good night depending on the time of day."

"That's exactly what Mom says when she comes home at nights," said Joah.

"Speaking of Mom, I think I hear her SUV in the driveway," declared Dad.

Madelyn ran to the front door and Joah peeped out the kitchen window.

"It's Mom! And she has pizza!" he yelled as he too rushed outside.

"Grandpa and Grandma sent us a Kindle," said Joah as he stretched out his hands for the pizza box.

"The box is hot," Mom said trying to avoid bumping into him.

"And a book too!" shouted Madelyn.

"What kind of book?" asked Mom.

It's a Virgin Islands cultural book," responded Joah.

"That sounds interesting," said Mom as she entered through the front door. "We can continue with the book after dinner," suggested Mom.

Then Joah, Madelyn, Mom and Dad all enjoyed cheesy chicken and broccoli pizza.

After the pizza dinner, they all sat in the living room. Mom sat in Dad's Lazy Boy chair while Dad and the children sat on the sofa.

"I will read Dad's sentences," suggested Mom as she put the recliner in the seating position.

Madelyn found her place and resumed reading her sentences.

O is for Okra fungi (pronounced fun-gee.)

Okra Fungi

"Okra fungi is boiled okra and cornmeal sautéed with vegetable oil and salt to a consistency similar to mashed potatoes. Then it is rolled into balls and served with sea foods, such as fish, conch and lobster. Okra fungi with boiled fish is one of the islands most popular dishes."

"Growing up on the island of St. Thomas, I can remember eating this dish every Friday night," declared their mom. "Most people eat it with boiled fish in butter sauce," she continued as she licked her lips recalling the buttery taste.

Madelyn and Joah watched each other, smiled, and then refocused on the reading.

"P is for… What's that word?" she asked her mother.

"Pis-sar-ro," pronounced her mom.

"Ca-mille Pis-sar-ro," said Madelyn.

Photo Credit: www.wikiart.org/camillepissarro
(Public Domain)

Camille Pissarro

"That's excellent!" said her mother as she read her section.

"Camille Pissarro, a painter, was born in 1830 on the island of St. Thomas. As a young boy, he demonstrated a great interest in painting. At age 22 he left the Virgin Islands to pursue an art career in France. He is remembered as one of the impressionist painters of his time."

"The Pissarro house is now a historical building on the island of St. Thomas," announced Dad.

"When you all visit next summer, you can ask to see this historical building," inserted Mom.

Joah and Madelyn nodded in agreement. Then Madelyn continued, "Q is for... How do you pronounce this word?" asked Madelyn.

"Quel- be," pronounced her mom.

"That's a hard word," declared Joah. "What does it mean?"

"Quelbe is a melting of African rhythms and chants blended with European music," read their mom. "Since the enslaved Africans were forbidden to play their own music, they adopted the music and dance of their masters but, with African rhythms and melodies. This unique blend led to a new native music known today as Quelbe."

Quelbe Dancers, EWES Dancers.

"It's a mixing of two kinds of music?" asked Joah. "Something like Hip Hop and Reggae mixed together?"

"Yes, you could say it's something like that," answered his mom chuckling softly.

Mom found her place, pushed her glasses on her nose and continued reading.

"In 2003, the 25th Legislature of the Virgin Islands passed a bill designating Quelbe as the official music of the US Virgin Islands. Governor Charles W. Turnbull signed the bill requiring that Quelbe be taught in the public schools."

"Do you and Mom know how to dance to this music?" asked Joah.

Illustration by: Ginelle Encarnacion

"Of course!" answered his mom as she sprang out of her chair and twirled around holding an imaginary skirt. Then she danced to the left and then to the right. Dad joined her and the two of them pranced around the bamboo center table laughing out loud.

Joah and Madelyn watched with bright eyes and wide smiles pasted on their faces.

Both parents tumbled onto the sofa laughing and embracing each other. "That sure brought back some ooooooooooooooooold time memories," said their dad.

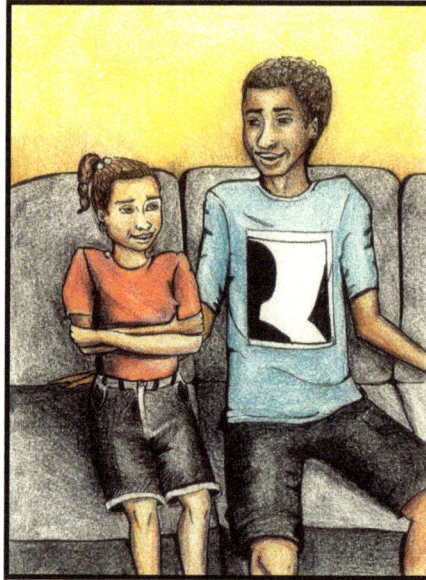

Illustration by: Ginelle Encarnacion

"It sure did," said their mom settling back into her chair.

"Continue reading Madelyn," said her dad as he settled back on the sofa.

Both children glanced at their parents, and then eyed each other, and then Madelyn found her place and began reading.

"R is for Red Gout."

"That's grout," corrected her dad as he leaned closer to see her book.

Red Grout

"Red grout is a fruit soup that was inherited from the Danes," her mom chimed in. "Guavas, tapioca, red food coloring and spices created this dish. Traditionally the Danes used strawberries and raspberries. When served thinly, it is called a soup and when served thickened it is called a dessert."

"Grandma made us this dessert, but I didn't know you can make soup with fruits," said Madelyn with a surprise look on her face.

"You can make soup with just about anything as long as it's tasty," said her mom as she found her place in the Kindle and continued.

"Red grout was the dessert eaten to celebrate the transfer of the islands from Denmark to the United States. Virgin Islanders enjoy this dessert especially during Christmas time."

"Can we visit Grandma and Grandpa for Christmas?" Madelyn begged.

"That's a great idea, Madelyn," Mom said. "Dad and I will discuss it and see if we can go this year, but if not, we will plan to go another Christmas so you can participate in St. Croix's Carnival."

Madelyn sprang up and hugged her mom.

Then she read, "S is for Salt Pond."

"In earlier days St. Johnians – that's what they call a native of St. John- obtained free salt from natural salt pond reservoirs that were all over the islands," continued Mom. "Salt ponds protect the coral reefs."

Salt Pond, Picture by Gerald Singer, VI.

"What's a coral reef?" asked Madelyn with a confused look on her face.

"We learned about coral reefs in science class," answered Joah. "It's like a rock that is found in the ocean. When all the coral polyps grow up together, they form like a mountain or ridge on the ocean floor," explained Joah.

Madelyn nodded and declared, "A mountain in the bottom of the ocean. Wow!"

"Why don't you make a list of all the unfamiliar words?" said Dad gesturing to Joah to find pen and paper in the drawer.

"Salt ponds serve as cushions between land and sea," Mom continued. "The ponds collect soil and fragments before they wash into the ocean. Salt Ponds in the US Virgin Islands are protected by the government."

"T is for Tim-o-thy Duncan", read Madelyn.

"Timothy Theodore Duncan is one of the Virgin Islands

most famous athletes," read Mom. He was born on the island of St. Croix on April 25, 1976.

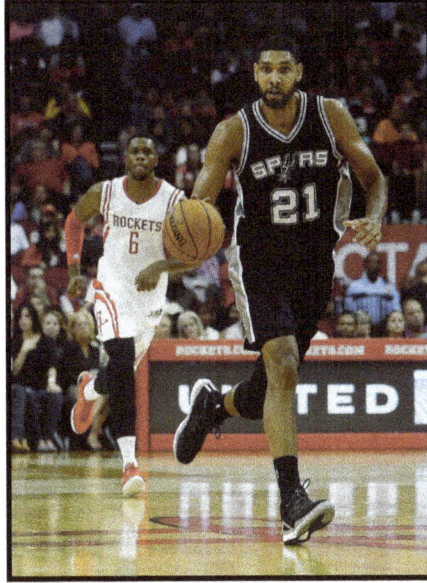

Photo Credit: Getty Images

Tim Duncan

In 1997 he was drafted into the National Basketball Association."

"I didn't know there were players from the Virgin Islands in the NBA,"said Joah.

"Yes, there are a few of them," said his father as he made a note on the research list.

"Wow! That's great!" said Joah as he waited for his mom to continue.

"He led his team, the San Antonio Spurs, to become five time NBA Champions. At the height of his career, he earned the NBA's Most Valued Player award."

Mom then motioned for Madelyn to read her section.

"U is for the U-ni-ver-si-ty of the Virgin Islands," read Madelyn.

University of the Virgin Islands, Picture permission given by UVI.

"The University of the Virgin Islands began as the College of the Virgin Islands in 1962," continued Mom. "At first the college only offered Associate degrees. However, in 1967 the bachelor's degree programs were added. The first master's degrees in Education were awarded in 1976 and two years later master's degrees in business and public administration were instituted.

The College of the Virgin Islands was renamed the University of the Virgin Islands in 1986."

Looking at her page, Madelyn yelled, "Look at the pretty cake! I want one just like this for my birthday," she said pointing to the book.

"I bet that's a Vienna cake. Oh so delicious!" Dad said smacking his lips.

"Dad got it right," said Mom.

Vienna Cake

Scrolling down the Kindle, Mom read, "V is for Vienna Cake. This cake looks like a colorful rainbow because of its fillings of guava, guava berry, pineapple and green lime marmalade. During the Christmas season, traditional foods are prepared. One traditional Christmas dessert is the Vienna cake. Family and friends who visit during festival time ask for this rich traditional cake. The Vienna cake is a recipe that was adopted from the Danes who once occupied the islands from 1733 to 1917."

"Can you make me a cake like this for my birthday?" asked Madelyn.

"I'll get the recipe from Grandma and make it for your next birthday," said her mom.

"Woo! Whoo!" sang Madelyn as she glanced at her brother.

"I will make one for your birthday too Joah, if you want," said Mom assuring both children.

Joah smiled and signaled for Madelyn to read her sentence.

"W is for Whim Mu-se-um," read Madelyn.

"Whim is the oldest sugar estate in the Virgin Islands," read Mom. "After its restoration in 1962, it was turned into a museum and opened to the public. The museum consists of the great house, the cookhouse, a bathhouse, and several cane processing machines.

The permanent exhibits depict the daily life of the people who worked and lived on plantations during the 1800's."

Whim Museum,
Picture permission given by STX Landmarks.

"I can remember visiting the museum during class trips," said their mom. "We always stopped by the cook house for local sweet treats."

"What kind of treats did you get?" asked Madelyn.

"I can remember eating benyes, and Vienna cake for sure," said Mom.

"Mmmm, said Madelyn licking her lips. "I wish we had some now."

"You will get these treats and more when you all visit," said Dad.

"I can't wait!" yelled Joah as he leaned his head back on the sofa.

Then Dad signaled for Mom to continue reading.

"Virgin Islanders and visitors are given a tour of the grounds and this helps islanders and visitors to understand the history of the islands."

"Let me read the last three words," said Mom. "These last words might be hard for you to pronounce."

"X is for Xebec" (pronounced ze beck), continued Mom. "Pirates travelled the Caribbean in xebecs. They roamed the waters of the Virgin Islands robbing cargo from vessels on the high seas.

Illustration by: Ange-Joseph-Antoine Roux (Public Domain)

Xebec

"I remember the pirates in the movie," said Madelyn. "Remember Mom?"

"Yes," said Mom making eye contact with Madelyn.

"Xebecs are small three- masted ships with both square and triangular sails. The ability for speed even when loaded made them perfect pirate ships."

"Y is for Yellow Breast," read Mom.

"Look! Look!" yelled Madelyn pointing to the bright yellow bird on the page. "When I visit Grandma Clarice and Grandpa Vincent, I'm going to climb the hills to catch a bird just like this!" she said pointing at the page.

Yellow Breast Bird, Picture by Gerald Singer, VI.

"You really can't catch them that easily. You'll have to just settle for admiring them," said Mom as she found her place in the Kindle.

"The Yellow Breast or Bananaquit (Coreba Flaveola) is a common bird that can be found throughout the Caribbean. It is between 4-5 inches long. Because of its curved bill, black back and yellow breast, it is easy to identify. It is also known as the 'Sugar Bird.' In 1970 the Yellow Breast was named the official bird of the US Virgin Islands."

"Z is for Zulus," continued Mom.

"The Zulus are a traditional Virgin Islands carnival troop. Their costumes consisted of black long johns, and white turban head pieces. Large earrings, nose rings, and armbands made from tin cans decorated their bodies."

"He looks just like the man on the Discovery Channel," declared Joah.

"Actually," said Mom, "The Zulu masqueraders came from our African ancestry. During carnival celebrations on the islands, some troop organizers described people and places from Africa."

"Why don't you add the Zulus to the research list?" said Dad as he made eye contact with Joah.

Joah grabbed his pen and notepad and wrote the new word.

"They used tallow grease, combined with soot to paint their skin," continued Mom. "In their hands they carried wooden hatchets with sliver painted blades."

"The first recorded appearance of the Zulus is in 1893 when they masqueraded through the towns on Christmas Second Day, and other holidays."

"Christmas second day is the day after Christmas," inserted Dad.

Modern Zulus at Virgin Islands Carnival,
Picture by Walter Bostwick, VI.

"The traditional Zulus, however, did not survive as a carnival troop in the Virgin Islands."

"Why didn't they survive as a carnival troop?" asked Joah.

"I am not sure," said Mom reflectively. "Maybe it brought back too many painful memories of our past, or maybe the costumes were not colorful enough. Most masqueraders liked colorful costumes."

"I want a colorful costume too," announced Madelyn. "And I want to be in carnival."

"It's called playing Mas," said her mother embracing.

"Maybe you and your brother want to see some old photos of your mother and me playing Mas?" Dad asked rising.

"Can we?" Joah beamed. "I am glad Grandma and Grandpa sent us this history lesson. I learned so much about the Virgin Islands. I enjoyed learning about my heritage."

"Me too," clapped Madelyn. "But I wish I had a benye right now."

Before anyone could respond, Mom said, "Look! The benye recipe is in the Kindle too."

"Let me see!" said their dad stretching closer.

"I guess we'll be making benyes for breakfast," said Joah with a huge smile on his face.

"I can't wait for tomorrow!" shouted Madelyn closing her book.

Illustration by: Ginelle Encarnacion

CRITICAL THINKING
AND RESEARCH QUESTIONS

1. Who was Hodding Carter? What do you think Carter meant by "roots and wings?" Discuss your ideas in small groups then report back to the class.

2. Research the life of Alton Augustus Adams Sr. Report your discoveries to the class.

3. Why do you think the early Virgin Islands musicians made flutes or fifes out of bamboo sticks?

4. Why do you think the Danes used strawberries and raspberries instead of guavas to make red grout?

5. Research about the life of David Hamilton Jackson. Write a page report. Make an oral presentation to the class, and be sure to include visuals.

6. Alexander Hamilton was shot in a duel. Find out who shot him. When was he shot and why?   Put on your detective hat. What clues did you find? Working with a partner, develop a visual time-line chart. Present your findings to the class.

7. Research what year the clinic on St. John was dedicated to Ms. Keating Smith. Who made the presentations?

8. Explain how salt ponds help to protect the eco system.

9. Identify the names of one salt pond on St. Croix and one on St. Thomas.

10. What native foods have you tasted? Which is your favorite and why?

BENYE RECIPE

1	package active dry yeast
1	cup hot water
4	cups all-purpose flour
½	teaspoon ground cinnamon
½	teaspoon ground cardamom (optional)
½	teaspoon ground nutmeg
	few drops banana essence
½	teaspoon mace
½	cup sugar
1 ½	teaspoon grated orange peel
7/8	cup mashed banana (very ripe)
2	tablespoons margarine, melted
	oil for frying

In large bowl combine yeast, flour, spices, orange peel and sugar. Add melted margarine to hot water. Gradually add dry ingredients. Beat for a minute or two. Add Mashed bananas and mix well.

Cover with a towel and set aside to rise until double in quantity. Batter should be medium soft. Drop by the spoonful into hot oil. Fry until brown. Drain on absorbing paper. Serve warm. Serves 36.

GLOSSARY

1. Correspondence classes: classes or instructions offered through the mail.

2. Impressionist painters: painters using this style emphasized light and colors to give an overall impression of their subject. Impressionism began in France near the end of the 19th century.

3. Kallaloo bush: Bata- Bata, Pulsey, Whitie Mary, Bower, and Papalolo. These leaves can be found growing wild in open fields.

References

- Adams, Alton A., and Mark Clague. *The Memoirs of Alton Augustus Adams, Sr.: First Black Bandmaster of the United States Navy*. Berkeley: University of California, 2008. Print.

- Bareuther, Carol. *Virgin Islands Cooking*. St. John, USVI: American Paradise Pub., 1994. Print.

- Bostwick, Walter. "Modern Zulus*" VI Source*. n.d. VI Source St. Croix Web. 16 Mar, 2015.

- Cancryn, Addelita. *Man of Vision*. St. Thomas, Virgin Islands. St. Thomas Graphics. 1975.

- Christian, Bradley. Assistant Director. St. Croix Cultural Heritage Inst. Telephone interview. 10 May 2010.

- Clarke, Clarice C., Valerie Combie Ph. D., and Kwame N. Garcia, State Director. *Virgin Islands Holiday Cooking*. Vol. 8. St. Croix, V.I.: Cooperative Extension Service, University of the Virgin Islands, 2005. Print.

- Dog Media Limited, Wagging. *Lemon Grass*. Photograph. Free Digital Photos.net, London, United Kingdom.

- Hoffman, Robert. *Alexander Hamilton: The Founding Father's Boyhood on the Island of St. Croix*. Christiansted, USVI: Southern Cross Publications, 2009. Print.

- Moolenaar, Ruth. *Profiles of Outstanding Virgin Islanders*. St. Thomas: Government of the U.S. Virgin Islands ESEA Title III Department of Education, 1969. Print.

- NBA Media Venture, LLC. "Tim Duncan Where Amazing Happens." *NBA.com*. Web. 13 Jan. 2010.

- Nicholls, Robert W. *Old-time Masquerading in The US Virgin Islands*. St Thomas, Virgin Islands: Virgin Islands Humanities Council, 1998. Print.

- Photograph. Seestjohn.com, Virgin Islands. *Seestjohn. com*. Ed. Gerald Singer. Web. 24 Apr. 2013.

- Taras, Mike. Caribbean Printing & Marketing Digital. mike@cpmvi.com 2015.

- United States. *Ronald Reagan Presidential Library*. National Archives and Records Administration. Web. 26 Apr. 2013.

- University of the Virgin Islands. 15 Sep. 2010. Web.

- "Whim Museum." St. Croix Landmarks Society Estate Museum St. Croix Landmarks Society. Web. 20 Oct. 2010.

- Willocks, Harold W. L. *The Umbilical Cord: The History of the United States Virgin Islands from Pre-Columbian Era to the Present*. St. Croix, Virgin Islands: Author, 1995. Print.

- "Xebec." Wikipedia. Wikimedia Foundation. n.d. Web. 18 Feb 2015.

www.ingramcontent.com/pod-product-compliance
Lightning Source LLC
La Vergne TN
LVHW010314070426
835509LV00023B/3477